I CHOOSE BREAKTHROUGH

Genesis 38: The Testimony of Tamar

JON RAFEAL SHORTEREZ

EXPECTED END

X

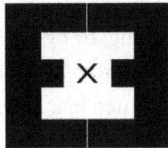

ENTERTAINMENT

Published by Expected End Entertainment/EX3 Books
www.EX3Books.com
ISBN: 0-9968932-1-0
ISBN-13: 978-0-9968932-1-3
Printed in the United States of America

DEDICATION

This book is dedicated to Courtney; we breakthrough together.
And to my mother Mary Colemon, a true example of fortitude and strength.

BOOK ENDORSEMENTS

"I Choose Breakthrough" is an honest, yet powerful exposition of Genesis 38. This book is a "MUST READ" for all who craves the incredible life of vision and purpose that God has intended. Jon's writing is both inspirational and revelatory. Pick up a copy today! You won't be sorry.

Derrick Traylor, author of Discover Your Power,
Senior Pastor of Love City Church, Humble, Texas

I Choose Breakthrough is a book of DELIVERANCE. Those who read it and open up their spirits to receive the impartation that will be imparted through the revelation in this book will receive a personal breakthrough. This book will challenge your thinking and revolutionize the way you look at Tamar's life. Revelation of her life will bring freedom to the lives of others that read it. This book should be one that you use for your personal arsenal and placed in your personal library.

Brandon Cornelius, Sr. Pastor
Spirit Life Training Center, Jackson, MS

This book is extremely relevant to the conditions society faces today. Lost identity is at crisis proportion! I believe that the Lord inspired Jon Rafeal to write about this dire reality, and I encourage everyone to read it and pray to overcome.

Pastor Maxine Gray
The Exodus Assembly, Jackson, MS

What a powerful expression of how we play a part of our destiny simply by making a choice. This book will reveal what you think about you and if your thoughts are His thoughts of you. You can have everything He wants for you, if you embrace I Choose Breakthrough.

Pastor Nathan Smith
Restoration House South, Bowling Green, VA

CONTENTS

Foreword - Bishop Brenda Kay Perry   i

1   Change Your Situation   1

2   Er   5

3   Onan "The Pullout Method"   15

4   I Can't Go Back   23

5   Promise of Shelah   27

6   Process of Time   33

7   Divine Opportunity to Change   49

8   Tamar Conceives With Judah   63

9   There's Something about Tamar   75

10   It's Time to Go   87

11   About the Author   93

FOREWORD

Fire is the aim of these pages. Fire not only brings heat but it also provides light. This is what is experienced while reading the story of Tamar through the eyes of this preacher.

It is evident through this book that God's creation was never designed to be crushed by the struggles of life. When we develop a proper perspective of our trials we inevitably discover divine training to walk out our purpose. As a pastor for 18 years, I have witnessed many souls go through bad situations and setbacks in their life. The greatest moments of my pastoral ministry is witnessing the testimony of breakthrough in the lives of God's chosen people.

There is no doubt that what you have experienced in your life gives you some hint as to what God desires to do through you. As you read this book, you can see how God takes an unimaginable situation and unfolds it to be in His divine will. Journeying through the pages, you will be captured in seeing yourself in place of Tamar.

The author has found a way to transmit the very heartbeat of God through the pages of this book. May you be encouraged and know that the Father's love for you is greater than any obstacle you could ever face.

Bishop Brenda K. Perry

New Life Temple Church

Houston, TX

1
CHANGE YOUR SITUATION

Growing up, many of us have often heard the phrase "play the hand that you have been dealt" in reference to a situation or condition. I propose that life is not the total of one hand but of several hands. There are many opportunities given to us where we can alter the outcome of what was initially considered our portion or lot in life. What you do with your cards in each hand or stage of life, defines who you are and the legacy you choose to leave behind. In other words, we may not have chosen to be born but we do choose how we will live. Many people have been born in some of the worst possible conditions but they made a choice to do what was necessary in order to better themselves. In life, we will have many obstacles to overcome and giants to fight. Some things are most certainly out of your control but that doesn't mean you will be dominated by it. You have more options than silently struggling in positions with people who would rather see you beneath what God has called you to. The option presented in this small book is the route of breakthrough!

Genesis 38 is perhaps one of the most interesting and intriguing passages of scripture in the Bible. For those who have read and studied the story of Joseph, you will find that Genesis 38 seems to be an interruption or even a digression from Joseph being sold into slavery. What makes this particular chapter so special is that within its verses we are quickly introduced to many characters without much background information or history of their development. We are not provided with the motives behind some of the characters' actions and are left, in most cases, with the responsibility to fill in the gaps of some ambiguous terminology and situations. The reader enters this chapter with the sense that a great scene is already in progress and you must catch up on what has taken place. One might even question the purpose of this chapter because it seems so random. Throughout the history of the church, not much attention has been given to Genesis 38. Many preachers and teachers rarely delve into the hidden treasures that are woven within the rich experience of Tamar. Despite its lack of exposure, in this chapter we can still see the redemptive plan of Christ, applications to be used in everyday living, and a powerful testimony that is sure to encourage all its readers. This book is only a small portion of some of the major themes displayed in the chapter.

Every preacher will tell you that they have their favorite texts to preach. It is their favorite because God will continue to download information, instruction, and inspiration long after the sermon is over. Genesis 38 has become great encouragement to me and all those who have been blessed by the testimony in Genesis 38. It is my prayer that as we take a look at this chapter that we are able to embrace the revelation and daily application that is still relevant today.

2
ER

> *Genesis 38:6-7 – "Then Judah took a*
> *wife for Er his firstborn, and her*
> *name was Tamar. But Er, Judah's*
> *firstborn, was wicked in the sight of*
> *the LORD, and the LORD killed him."*

When we begin to take a look at what transpires in the beginning of the chapter, we find that Judah has arranged a marriage between his first born son Er and a woman named Tamar. This, in and of itself, is a normal event but we find that God removes Er because of his wickedness. It is unclear as to what Er's sin or iniquity is but it displeased the Lord to the point that scriptures says God killed him.

Without assuming or adding to the text, it is interesting to note that the name Er is where we develop the English word 'error'. In other words, Tamar is connected to a man whose name means mistake, to stray, or to err. Everyone has been in the position of Tamar at one point in time. We all have made mistakes and have been connected to people who turned out to be mistakes. Whether it be in school, marriage, ministry, relationships, or even career choices, there has been plenty of mistakes. Er in the text is symbolic of the spirit of error.

In regards to relationships, we must be careful of whom we come into covenant agreement with. Many times, we quickly align ourselves with things and people who at first glance may look good or beneficial but in the long run could prove to be a hindrance to purpose. We must get to a point where we properly weigh a thing before connecting in order to avoid feelings of bitterness and regret. This is an important principle for all aspects of life. Marriages end in swift divorce or separation simply because it was entered into without proper counseling or prayer. No one is exempt from making mistakes or even from poor choices. You have to be determined to push past them. The enemy wants so desperately for you to stay stuck on past failures. He knows that God has great plans for your life and would rather you stay ignorant of future success by solely focusing on your mistakes. In this stage of your life, you cannot play into the hand of the enemy by consistently sulking in defeat or "mess ups". God is calling you beyond your last mistake! If you are reading this, you are still here and greater is still available to you. Your mistake was not big enough to derail the purpose of God on your life. The blood of Jesus covers the mistakes and causes them to be used as learning experiences.

The blessing and good news from Tamar's experience with Er is that before she could have a baby by him, God removed him. God did not allow Tamar to become pregnant by the mistake! It is indeed a blessing that God would not allow you to carry around the fruit of your mistakes. Guilt, bitterness, and regret are all fruit of mistakes. Once a mistake has penetrated your mind and heart it can take years to overcome. The person who is pregnant and carrying around grief and regret will never truly experience deliverance from the past. Once bitterness is conceived it brings forth stagnation. With God however, you can overcome the pain of the past right now. His grace and mercy causes us to push beyond the mistake in order to fully embrace who we are. Through the blood of Christ, you are not defined by what you have done or who you were once connected to. You are defined by God's purpose for your life. I declare that you are not married to your failure; you are submitted to God.

Many times in basketball when a player makes a mistake while passing the ball or after missing a shot, they drop their head and get down on themselves. A good basketball coach on the sideline will scream, "Get back on defense!" because the play is not over. Your one mistake or missed shot is not the end of the world. You still have an opportunity to get the ball back and win the game. Everyone will make plenty of mistakes in life but it is how we respond to those "mess ups" that ultimately define who we are.

Now let's clarify the difference between error and disobedience. An error or mistake happens from sloppy or hasty decisions. When one fails to properly prepare for a test they may miss several questions. An error can occur from receiving and applying incorrect knowledge. This can lead to unfavorable results. Error is primarily the result of ignorance. Ignorance simply means you did not know something so therefore you erred. What many call a mistake may actually be disobedience. To disobey implies to know and understand yet choose to go against what is being said or done. For instance, it is no mistake that you went to a bar and got drunk. Neither can you slip up and have sex with someone. These are both rebellious choices that go against the Word and Will of God. While it is important to differentiate between error and disobedience, it is equally important that we understand that they both lead to the same destination; failure.

Error is a spirit that is oftentimes transferred from parent to child or from generation to generation. It is no secret or surprise that you can only impart what you possess. Those who have raised you can only teach or show you what they themselves were taught. What if the knowledge they passed on was not accurate. Just think, for some, the way they process information, enter into business agreements, and maintain intimate relationships could be based on their parents' past hurts and failures. The spirit of error can cause you to operate in your parents' fear of things that you have never actually experienced. If this is true then your entire perspective and understanding has a high chance of being twisted. The spirit of error causes one to live a limited life because of incorrect knowledge.

Perhaps the most significant and obvious example of this would be the history of slavery in America. Because of incorrect knowledge from greedy slave masters and land owners, many generations of African-Americans were and still are disenfranchised. The systematic breakdown of the mind of the slave and generational transfer of self-degradation has crippled millions in America. When one's mindset is wrapped around false self-knowledge about their lifestyle, it becomes contrary to the intentions of God.

In order to get rid of error, you must embrace the truth of God and His word. The truth of God comes to bring direction, correction, and revelation knowledge to your life.

Without it, you will experience many pitfalls and setbacks. St. John 17:17 says, *"Sanctify them in the Truth; your word is truth"* (ESV). In other words, it is the Word of God that sets you apart from destruction and downfall. There is a way that seems right unto a man but the end thereof is destruction (Proverbs 14:12). Thy Word is a lamp unto my feet and a light unto my pathway (Psalm 119:105). The Word of God comes to bring illumination. It sheds light on every thought and intention of the heart. Error brings darkness, but the light of God's truth will cause you to see every obstacle that would cause you to stumble. So, in order to apply the truth of God to our lives we must look at the results of past decisions. Ask yourself why do you believe what you believe and then measure that to the Word of God. I call this cutting the Light on. We all have access to this great God of light (James 1:17 ESV) but many of us walk in darkness. The Spirit of Error can affect every area of your life. It can ruin relationships, finances, careers, and even churches. The solution to error is the Truth of God. If error is in your house, allow God to get rid of it. Gen. 38:7 says that the Lord put ER to death because he was wicked. God wants to eliminate every wrong way of thinking that has helped to hinder your forward progress. He even wants to remove those individuals who are "Ers" in your life. The blessing is that God does not hold your past mistakes over your head. His power is like a giant eraser that removes the stain and residue of past failures and bad decisions from you.

In order to move on from Er, there must be a healing of the mind. The results of mistakes can scar us mentally and emotionally. Sometimes it may seem impossible to move beyond how people hurt you or mistreated you. It is hard to recover from certain positions you thought would be a benefit to you. You must be healed in order to trust again and not enter into new relationships or new opportunities with hurt from the past. God will introduce you to new, purposeful people but if you are still hurt from your past you will run from new, God-ordained connections. In order to truly be healed you have to admit where you are and own what has taken place in your life. All too often we live in fantasy land when it comes to things we have done or bad experiences that have happened to us. While we do not relive the past we must acknowledge those mistakes (Er) in order to bury them. Yes, learn from your mistakes then bury them because you will not connect with Er again. Surely at some point there had to be a proper burial for Er. At one point your old way of doing things and way of thinking was a terrible reality. Now, God is bringing you to a greater understanding of who you are so that you can learn from where you have been and embrace where He is leading you.

Error is not the end of you! God's plan for your life is not derailed or ruined because you connected with Er. Please know that you will make mistakes but like Tamar, do not stay married to error. It's time to put Er in your rearview mirror. Once Er is behind you, you will see that your purpose is still intact and God's mind about you has not changed.

JON SHORTEREZ

3
ONAN:
"THE PULLOUT METHOD"

> *Genesis 38:8-10 – Then Judah said to Onan, "Go in to your brother's wife and perform the duty of a brother-in-law to her, and raise up offspring for your brother." But Onan knew that the offspring would not be his. So whenever he went in to his brother's wife he would waste the semen on the ground, so as not to give offspring to his brother. And what he did was wicked in the sight of the LORD, and he put him to death also.*

After the death of Er, Tamar is then connected with Er's brother, Onan. The scripture says anytime Onan would sleep with Tamar, he would pull out of her and release his seed on the ground. Onan is symbolic of every individual that causes a good feeling but does not want the responsibility of helping you to produce. They are the ones who enable you to do things that bring no manifestation of the promise of God for your life. Onan is not one who lacks ability. He has all of the right equipment to make a baby but refuses to release what is necessary to get pregnant. This person simply doesn't want to "go all the way" with you because he/she knows they will not get all the credit for what will happen. We are in a time where people do not think about helping one another. Many are so consumed with their own gain and pleasure that they overlook individuals right next door who are in unfortunate situations. Onan has seed but chooses to waste it. What is seed symbolic of? Onan's seed is symbolic of time, money, energy, ideas, and resources. If there is going to be change, you must find people who will invest and release seed in your life. Therefore, it is important to properly identify any and all Onans in your circle. When you truly desire change for the better, you must examine the fruit of every relationship. If they are not a benefit or a necessity, they might be a hindrance to your progress. Some relationships may bring a good feeling but do not help you to produce or operate in what God called you to. The fact that Onan would rather waste his seed than to raise a son in his brother's name shows that he is selfish and irresponsible. Anytime you are connected to a selfish individual, you will find that you are always the one left feeling empty and unfulfilled. All Onan wants is the thrill of the moment and to simply go through the motions as if he is working to produce. It is from these people that you must separate to experience positive change.

Onan will drain you of your energy and strength.

Leaving you with nothing to show for your time spent with him. The only influence Onan has over you is a temporary good feeling. Onan represents people who will stroke your ego so that you will continue to do what makes them happy. They are enablers who contribute to you being stuck in bad habits. Onan is a manipulator that is not easily detected because every time you are around them there is some sense of relief or a sort of "high". When they are gone, however, the music stops, the lights come on and you are left to clean up the mess. We should all seek to connect with people who leaves you feeling full of power, hope, and determination. Connect to these people. God will ordain people that will empower you to do great things. Leave Onan alone. He leaves you tired and empty! Your greatest enemy is not the one who agitates you or brings irritation. Your most difficult foe is the one who brings you pleasure without production. Identify Onan and then disconnect!

Onan in the church

In many ways the church has become just like Onan. It wants to feel good but does not want the responsibility of raising a baby. We are in a state of deception when we look for our pleasure at the expense of God's plan. The assignment of the church is to bring glory to the name of the Lord. In verse 8, we have an example of how the church would be in the last days. Its main focus is pleasure while neglecting its purpose. We have created an atmosphere of people who feel "good" about going to the local church as long as the preached Word does not challenge or rebuke us. The churches of our day have become pleasure houses, where we expect to be entertained instead of empowered. So many people leave services the same way they came and ultimately forfeit their God-given assignment to produce for the Kingdom of God. Onan's agenda in his relationship to Tamar was to receive but never contribute. The language of the text suggests that Onan had intimate relations with Tamar several times. This is how many approach God. They seek only what He is able to do and how good he can make them feel. The church that Jesus established was not a feel good church infested with selfish individuals who seek their own gain. The church has too many Onans. When Onan is in the pulpit, he provides a temporary sensation of euphoria without equipping souls to impact the Kingdom. When Onan leads praise and worship, they blindly escort people through a list of their favorite songs instead of singing what God desires to be heard. Onans in the congregation will always complain about church issues but never contribute any solutions. It's about time we expel the spirit of Onan from the church.

The Bible says that Jesus is our elder brother and it is in His name that we are able to do great things. We have access to heavenly places and an entrance into the grace of God through the blood and the name of Jesus. We are instructed in Colossians 3:17 to do everything in the name of Jesus. This is a very interesting and powerful scripture. Paul gives us the most important tip to access and operate in the Kingdom. If we preach, sing, dance, or write, it should all be done in His name and for His glory. Too many today seek to put their names and initials on ministries and movements. Jesus gets all the glory because He shed his blood for us. He is the author of salvation and the chief cornerstone of the church.

Verse 9 says that Onan knew that the child would not be his so he wasted his seed on the ground. This speaks to all of us who consider ourselves servants of God. We have gifts and talents that were given to us by God and for His purpose. We cannot allow our pride and selfishness to waste or withhold what He gave us. If you are truly submitted to the Lordship of Jesus then your gifts, talents, time, finances, and abilities are submitted as well. The ground can't do anything with the seed or sperm of a man. The question is not whether or not you are gifted but are you using your gift in an area that can reap benefit from your release? According to Genesis 3:17, God cursed the ground because of Adam's sin. So the seed that was released from Onan to the ground was cursed. The church and the individuals that make up the corporate body of Christ cannot afford for our efforts to be cursed all because of misplaced seed. Our seed is spilled on the ground when we exalt our name and agenda above the name of Jesus. When we hold purposeless services only for the promotion of a person we waste our seed. The ground represents every cursed system or agenda that has not produced anything because it is not connecting with what God ordained. The seed was made for the womb just like your gifts and talents were made for the enrichment of the Kingdom. By offering your gifts to another opposing entity you release what is divinely given into a cursed system.

While saying the name of Jesus is important, it is more important to emphasize there is no substitute for operating in that name. When the Bible speaks of "in the name of Jesus", it means to live in the authority, power, and righteousness of Jesus. The name of Jesus is not a magic word or a secret esoteric code for a select few. It is a form of identification that gives us access into heavenly places and a weapon against the enemy. The declaration of the name must be backed up by a person's lifestyle. You can only expect the benefits that go along with the family name if you are actively living in the righteousness provided by the Lord and Savior. If or when the unsaved calls on the name of Jesus, it is for salvation, identification, and entrance into the Kingdom of God.

4
I CAN'T GO BACK

We must understand the significance of the death of Er and Onan. It seems that God's treatment of these two brothers was harsh or cruel. So, why did God kill them? God had to totally remove them and provide a way for Tamar to be delivered from them. He had to completely remove them from her life so that the next chapter in her story could begin. In some cases and areas in our lives, God will remove people and things in such a way that will eliminate all possibilities of you going back. God is sovereign enough to do things His way and He knows how to handle you and whatever situation you may be in. Many times if he doesn't cause a radical shift to move you forward, you will stay in unhealthy relationships and never break the negative cycle that has hindered you from advancing. The death of Er and Onan seems so outrageous and drastic and some would even suggest that surely it didn't take all that. I would like to suggest that the death of these individuals is not the point. It is the overall divine message that God will do things that we may not presently understand to push us in the right direction. For some, losing a job caused you to trust God for another one that ended up providing better pay, benefits, hours, and less stress. The death of Er and Onan represents a divine radical shift that interrupts the mundane unproductiveness in our lives. When we become blinded by our current state, God can and will shake us to a point where our eyes are opened to see that there is more of God and more that He has for us. Change and shift may be uncomfortable and definitely scary but trust in God that he is directing you to fulfillment and purpose.

The children of Israel experienced a similar occurrence when they crossed the red sea. The Bible says that the waters parted for them so that they could walk forward to the other side. When they got to the other side safely, the waters came back together in what had to have been a violent demonstration of God's power because it killed the Egyptians who were chasing them. When the waters came back together,, it not only eliminated their enemies but it kept them from returning or reconnecting to a land of bondage and slavery. God prepared a way for the exit, but never intended for them to go back. When God delivers you, understand that He will make provision for your exit and has no intentions for you to return to a dead person or a dead place. In order to get you over some things He has to make it "dead" to you. Some people are still alive but they are dead to you so that you will not remain distracted and delayed by them. It is your responsibility to resist the urge to try and resurrect dead things that God eliminated from you.

The burden of deliverance is on God, but the burden of freedom is on you. Freedom is to be maintained and is the responsibility of the one who has been delivered. In other words there are strategies, rules, and principles that need to be implemented and enforced as a safeguard against going back to bondage. Once God delivers, do not go back to Egypt. Many times we forfeit our freedom and progress because we are familiar and comfortable with people and places that God is trying to separate us from. It is not the will of God for you to be stuck, stagnate, and oppressed in the comfort of a familiar situation. Never allow comfort to cause you to dwell in a fruitless place.

5
PROMISE OF SHELAH

> *Gen. 38:11* – Then Judah said to
> Tamar his daughter-in-law, "Remain
> a widow in your father's house till my
> son Shelah is grown." For he said,
> "Lest he also die like his brothers."
> And Tamar went and dwelt in her
> father's house.

Many of us have gone through periods where we are angry with God because of tragic events that have taken place in our lives. It is this time that your faith is tested to the max. It is not something that you can ever truly be prepared for. This is when your mind will fail to find a way to reconcile what has happened to you. As humans, we tend to find ways to "self-soothe" during times of anguish and despair. There are familiar habits that we run to to pacify us through the pain. There is a stage in your life, however, where none of the usual methods will work. You will not find release in encouraging words from close friends or family and the antidote to your predicament seems an eternity away.

It would be natural and even expected for an individual to shut down and literally curl into a defensive ball.

Fortunately, when you have reached this point is when God will supernaturally give you the strength and fortitude to get through another day.

There are times in our lives where it may seem that every time we are close to something great it falls through. In this moment, it seems as if Tamar is cursed because everyone she becomes intimate with dies. Whatever your struggle may be please know that any curse over your life is broken because of the shed blood of Christ. You are not cursed you are being processed!

The adversary of your soul and purpose is always busy at work against you. One of Satan's greatest schemes is to make you feel weak and inadequate. In most cases, people feel helpless and hopeless because they have entertained a deceptive lie in their minds. The lie and the deception is that you will never get out of your father's house. Tamar has reached a period of her life where she is being sent back to her father's house. This is an example of a life in regression. Before she was chosen to be married to Er and eventually to Onan, her father's house was a place of protection, provision and security. Now, it has become a place of mourning. She has lost her husband in both marriages and now has to go through the grieving process.

By now, many people would start to believe that there is something wrong with Tamar. Maybe she is cursed. Maybe she had something to do with their deaths. Judah thought the problem was Tamar, when in fact the clash was between his wicked sons and the purpose of Tamar.

When people have no insight, speculation and false conjecture is inevitable. The real conflict had to do with her purpose. We must understand that God deals with us according to His plan for our lives. Every blessing, rebuke, friendship, and even enemies are assigned to you because of the intentions of God for you. You have to realize that you are not the problem. The friction comes when things and people around you do not line up with where you should be or with whom you should be. Anytime you connect with things and people that are not assigned to your purpose, there will be conflict with the God of your purpose. There is a struggle because we try to hold on to some things that God wants dead. You will never experience abundant life in Christ carrying around dead things. God is divinely setting you up to walk in purpose. He desires to disconnect you from ER and Onan so stop trying to resurrect the past. Allow Him to remove the hindrance and stop speaking life to dead useless things. We must be careful not to allow our struggle to persuade us into agreement with the enemy. You are in a delicate place mentally and the enemy knows it. Because of where you are and who you are, the enemy will deploy every weapon in his arsenal to cause you to believe you are powerless.

Tamar was in a place of stagnation waiting to be married to Shelah. This is a time and season where the mind games of the enemy starts. Whether a person is saved or unsaved, the mind is still the battlefield of your soul. We must guard our mind and thoughts at all times. We do this by protecting what goes in our eyes and ears. What we hear and see effects the way we think and believe. As a man thinks, so is he. So in order to get you to fall short of who God called you to be the enemy has to convince you to think beneath who you are. Whenever a negative thought or thoughts of fear and doubt pop into your mind you should remind yourself not to think beneath who you are. Some thoughts are beneath you. The enemy wants your mind to nurture and water negative seeds so that the results of your thinking will have you living a lie. Anytime you live beneath God's thoughts for you, you are living in a lie. God's thoughts and opinion of you is the ultimate truth. The only way to make sure you walk in truth is to become familiar with His Word. Your very own thoughts will work against you if your mind has not been washed with the

Word of God (Ephesians 5:26).

If you know that you have been in a stagnate place, you cannot become a slave to your feelings. When your feelings dictate your life, you become easily conquerable. Stagnation invites depression, bitterness, and strife. We can get so caught up in how we feel that we miss out on opportunities to move forward. Some people have been stuck in situations so long that they have gotten used to being abused, overlooked, broke, and misused. God did not create you to be a victim. It's time to tell a familiar problem that enough is enough and it is time for a change.

6
PROCESS OF TIME

---

*Gen. 38:12 – In the course of time the
wife of Judah, Shua's daughter, died.
When Judah was comforted, he went up
to Timnah to his sheepshearers, he and
his friend Hirah the Adullamite.*

The term process of time is an indication that a
considerable amount of time passed by in the life of Tamar.
So much time had passed that in one verse Shelah is too
young to marry but by now Tamar realizes that Shelah is
old enough but she has not yet been given to him for
marriage. Shelah is into his adulthood by the time she
realizes Judah has no intentions of honoring his word to put
her with his son. The promise of Shelah is what she held on
to as she went back to her father's house. She had
something to look forward to while she waited for a young
boy to became a man. Can you imagine how she must have
felt as she realized that she would never be put with
Shelah? It's only the promises of God that are yes and
Amen. In other words, man has the ability to fail and to lie
but God is not a man that He should lie. If He said a thing
then it will come to pass. Your destiny is between you and
God. Therefore, the only word you can wholeheartedly

depend on is the Word of God.

Without the Word of God as a compass for our lives we become vulnerable to manipulation from others who will distort your vision and cause inner conflict with what God placed in you. This is why many are confused concerning their purpose. What they received from God doesn't really agree with the so-called wisdom from another. Those who are operating in manipulation seek to control your direction by feeding you false information. People will give advice based on their selfish will for you or from their emotional connection to you. Manipulation can cause you to feel bad for leaving a situation or person. People who are being manipulated often suffer from lack of vision or lack of strategy for their purpose. Ultimately, manipulation works when you submit or subject yourself to another's opinion.

In order to be manipulated, you have to subvert or suppress the truth about who you truly are. Only the Spirit of God, which is the Spirit of truth, can break the stronghold of manipulation. It is the Spirit of God that provides the foresight, truth, and strength needed to break from the spell of someone else's opinion. If their advice or words do not line up with what God shows you then you may need to strictly filter what you receive from them. The Word of God will become your cover and from His word you will be able to start making positive verbal investments into your own spirit. Your dependability on the words of man will be a thing of the past as you grow more confident in the Word of God.

Understand and Adjust

Understanding brings adjustment. It is only when one understands their situation in relationship to their purpose that they are able to make the right and necessary adjustments for progress. The understanding that Tamar received awakened her to the fact that Shelah who was promised to her was fully grown and there were no plans or intentions for them to marry. Her understanding brought clarity to her life and caused her to stop waiting on Judah to make a move for her. It was clear that it was time for her to make a move for herself. It may be time for you to make a move but that will never happen until you get a true understanding of your situation. Once you understand and have clarity then you will make the correct moves that bring deliverance and help to maintain freedom. Oftentimes we make moves before understanding which only leads to "busy work". Busy work may look good but it only serves to make you tired and drained. Don't confuse busy work with progressive movement and advancement. Busy work is a term derived from school teachers. They would give the students assignments to keep them quiet and busy. Ultimately, the work would not be graded and would not be considered towards the overall advancement of the student. Once we receive proper understanding of who we are and where we are in relationship to our divine purpose, we can then do the work that counts and has meaning. Proverbs 4:5-9 instructs us to get wisdom and understanding, which will put you in prime position to make positive moves in your life.

Make more moves than announcements

Tamar didn't make an announcement or host some elaborate launch party before leaving her father's house. She simply made a move. All too often we make more announcements and social media posts about what we want to do instead of putting a plan in motion to accomplish whatever it is that God has placed in us to do. The action of a thing is more important than the announcement of it. If one continues to declare "deliverance is coming soon" but never sets out to do what it takes to be delivered, eventually people will conclude that that person is not worth listening to. Make more moves than announcements. Let your faith and progress speak for you.

There is no casual approach to deliverance. We cannot expect to just happen upon purpose. It takes deliberate aggressive action, well informed decisions, and careful planning. When a system has you trapped, you will need to become dedicated to deliverance and disciplined to stay free. Like many people, Tamar had been stuck in a familiar place. Anytime you have been in a place for a long period of time the thought of moving from there can be overwhelming.

There are two main evil spirits that are attracted to people of great purpose. It is the spirit of fear and spirit of heaviness. They can also be known as hindering spirits which come to block, stop, or delay the workings of God through you. It is in the "process of time" that you must deal with and overcome these things so that you can be free.

Spirit of Fear

It is the fear of the unknown that probably frightens us the most. The fear of the unknown is a major barrier that can prevent you from making progressive movements. Fear can cause us to misread and misinterpret things that come to make us better. It causes our vision to become blurry and leads to a misunderstanding of opportunities. Some people are frozen by fear of the unknown because it creates an unrealistic view of potential outcomes of a given situation. It clouds the mind and has the same effects on a person that is under the influence of alcohol. Fear sets in when one is unsure of the promises of God. When we doubt the power of God in our life, we become unsure of His leading and direction which causes us to settle for less or at best make tentative moves in life. The scriptures let us know in 2 Timothy 1:6-7,

> *"Wherefore I put thee in remembrance that thou stir up the gift of God, which is in thee by the putting on of my hands. For God hath not given us the spirit of fear; but of power, and of love, and of a sound mind."*

Having a sound mind is also known as having a sober mind with self-control and discipline. So, in order to get over fear you have to first recognize that fear does not come from God. God gives power and a clear, sound mind.

The mind is the governor of the body and is responsible for our thoughts, feelings, beliefs, and attitudes. If or when fear takes control of the mind, it then hijacks everything the mind is in charge of. Fear then becomes the dominate influence and will only negatively affect your God-given functioning.

Having a sober-mind is important for many reasons and is the difference maker for those who truly want to exit unhealthy situations. A sober-mind is a clear mind that is not easily swayed by the opinions of man. A sober-minded person has the clarity of perception to see the difference between constructive criticism and negative cynicism. Possessing and maintaining a sound mind is everything! Without it, you will not be able to properly identify your current status, assess your closest relationships, or even plan for your future. You need a sober mind in order to remember the word of God for your life. Holding on to what God said to you about you is so important! You can't allow the adversaries of your purpose to deter you, the concerns from your family and friends to confuse you, or even your own negative thoughts to cripple you. You can be sure that what God says about you will come to pass.

In 2 Timothy 1:6, Paul is encouraging Timothy to *"stir up the gift of God that is in him"*. In other words, we must recognize that God has placed gifts on the inside of each of us and it is the assignment of the enemy to keep us from operating in our gifts. There is a certain level of confidence that comes along with your gift. It is the simple fact that God placed it in you. The gifts that you possess did not come from some undependable, irresponsible, stranger. What you have in you comes directly from God Almighty, the creator and ruler of the universe. He is the one who formed and made you. The reason why God gave you the vision, plan, dream, or idea is because he can trust you with it. Furthermore, if the dream or vision is of God all you must do is overcome the spirit of fear and begin to do what he placed in you. The fear of failure may try to block you but remember Paul's instructions to Timothy. You have to stir up the gift. Fear wants you to hide and suppress your gift but you have to stir it up. Stirring up the gift means to cause it to come alive. Paul was referring to the way a person would stir up the coals of a dying fire in order to get that fire to grow again. Fear comes to smother the fire in you until eventually no one can benefit from the warmth, light, and power of the gift of God that resides in you. You must rebuke fear so that your fire will grow and be a blessing to all those who are connected to you!

Using your gift will bring blessings to you while you are being a blessing to the kingdom of God. The next time you feel afraid to operate in your passion, remember who placed it in you and operate boldly in your gift. Stir it up! You cannot become so concerned with what people may say to you or about you. You might as well operate in your God-given purpose because people are going to talk about you no matter what you do. When you see others who are fearful to move out of negative situations encourage them to operate boldly in their gift. So, to overcome fear, we first must recognize that God did not give us the spirit of fear. Then, we must stir up the gift that the spirit of fear is preventing us from moving or operating in. Walk in confidence knowing that it is God who placed it in you because He can trust you to be a blessing to his Kingdom.

The enemy knows that the gifts on the inside of you are also weapons against his kingdom of darkness. This is why the spirit of fear comes while you are in a stagnate place. He has to try to stop you from deploying your gifts. The devil wants you to doubt your gift, talents and abilities.

He wants you to speak against who you are, and to speak against your future.

Fear will even speak and mask itself as wisdom. The advice from fear will not line up with the word of God or His purpose for your life. Fear comes to provide an alternate, "safer" route that is contrary to the way of God. It will sabotage the operation of divine strategies and enable one to find justification for stagnation. The enemy comes to cause you to agree with your fears but God gives you the power to overcome your fear. The enemy uses fear to play mind games on the believer. Declare "game over" to the voice of fear! It is time now for us to become more confident in who we are and in the God we serve. Declare now that you will no longer listen or be submitted to the spirit of fear! Through the power of God, you will possess and maintain a sound mind!

Spirit of Heaviness

The spirit of heaviness is another hindering spirit that is closely connected to fear and may be a result of fear. Heaviness, which manifests as depression, can come from prolonged stagnation. The mixture of frustration and hopelessness is an invitation for the Spirit of heaviness.

This particular spirit causes one to have a grim and negative outlook on life. It slowly filters positive energy out of you by smothering you with the overwhelming feeling of despair. The spirit of heaviness is a trap that causes one to be completely weighed down and can even cause numbness to the voice of God. It is the lack of hope that causes a person not to put forth any effort to do better or change where they are in life. Procrastination, excessive sleeping, and isolation are just a few of the effects of the spirit of heaviness. The ultimate agenda or assignment of the spirit of heaviness is to keep you grounded so that you won't be able to have mobility. Its plan is to hold you hostage so that you will remain unproductive. In order to overcome the strong grip of heaviness you must fully submerge yourself in the word of God. It is the authority of His word that will cause the tentacles of heaviness to be loosed from your mind. In Psalm 42:11, David shows us how to encourage ourselves.

"Why are you downcast, O my soul? Why so disturbed within me? Put your hope in God, for I will yet praise him, my Savior and my God." Psalm 42:11

David gives a strategy or formula to overcoming heaviness. He speaks to himself. He tells himself to put hope and trust in God. As I have mentioned before, you have to remind yourself of who your God is. You have to talk to yourself in such a way that stirs you to victory and shakes you out of the grip of heaviness. There will be plenty of times where you will have to be your biggest motivator. In 1 Samuel 30:6, David had to encourage himself in the Lord his God. He was surrounded by people who were so upset with him that they wanted to stone him but he had a conversation within himself that caused him to remain strong. The word "encouraged" used in that text, is derived from the Hebrew word 'chazaq' which implies growing strong during an intense battle. It also means to take a firm hold in the midst of adversity. While breaking bad habits and generational cycles, you are in a battle for your life. Speaking to yourself is the means by which the word of God takes a firm hold and deep root in your soul. When you continue to rehearse and remind yourself of the word of God, you will become stronger and more determined when trials in your life arrive. Take a firm hold to the promises of God revealed through the Holy Scriptures and be encouraged that whatever is trying to stop you has no power over you.

Fear and heaviness both come to taint and confuse your mind about what God said. If this happens, you will speak negatively to yourself. Our hope is in the greatest power there is, which is Jesus. In Him there is no failure. Knowing this will eliminate hopelessness because all of your work and effort to advance in life starts and ends with Jesus. Philippians 1:6 says, *"And I am sure of this, that he who began a good work in you will bring it to completion at the day of Jesus Christ."* To put it plainly, we have hope in Jesus because he helps you to fulfill and complete the very thing he placed in you to do, which is your life's purpose.

The Chains of Comfort

Tamar could have simply stayed in her father's house. The fact that you know what will happen where you are makes things predictable and comfortable for you but is it what God has ordained for you? We cannot allow our present condition to make us blind to our own future. Comfortable is the womb of stagnation. So many people are stuck in a position that once provided them comfort and stability. The question is what do you do when a place of comfort and provision turns into a place of bondage? Before Egypt was ever a place of slavery for the Israelites, it was first a place of refuge and resources. Their prolonged stay there gave enough time for a pharaoh to rise up who wanted to enslave them. Had they continued progressively, they would have never had to endure the hardships of Egypt. We cannot afford to stay in a place long enough to see it gradually become bondage. What you are in right now is not the final chapter of your life. There is so much more room for you to grow. As long as there is breath in your body, God still has more in store for you. Having this particular mindset does not mean you can never be satisfied or that you are ungrateful but this mentality understands that the plan of God is far greater than anything we could ever imagine.

Isaiah 55:9 - For as the heavens are higher than the earth, so are my ways higher than your ways and my thoughts than your thoughts.

Ephesians 3:20 - Now to him who is able to do far more abundantly than all that we ask or think, according to the power at work within us.

In other words, the way to avoid being stuck because

of comfort is to understand that God always has more for you and it is far greater than you could ever imagine!

7
DIVINE OPPORTUNITY TO CHANGE

Gen. 38:13-14 – And it was told Tamar, saying, "Look, your father-in-law is going up to Timnah to shear his sheep." 1So she took off her widow's garments, covered herself with a veil and wrapped herself, and sat in an open place which was on the way to Timnah; for she saw that Shelah was grown, and she was not given to him as a wife.

It is the death of Judah's wife that provides an opportunity for Tamar to make an aggressive move concerning her situation. This is a defining moment in her life. Death has a way of causing the living to wake up. Death shows us exactly how fragile and precious life truly is. It brings all things into proper perspective. When death happens, it causes you to evaluate your life, or at least it should. In most cases, conviction will even take place if you have yet to begin operating in your God-given assignment. In other words, when death happens close to a person of understanding, it causes him to live more. We must get in a position that helps us to see more, do more, and grow more. Wake up! Do not allow your senses to become dull. Stay alert! God is trying to shift you. We cannot allow our current condition to put us to sleep and cause us to miss out on the full promises of God. As long as you are breathing, God is still working out His purpose for your life.

Tamar had to make a decision at this crucial point in her life. Do I stay here or do I make a move? To stay would lead to more wasted time and the only person to blame would be herself. It would obviously be less of a hassle to stay but most times deliverance will not be convenient. You will have to make some uncomfortable changes that may even defy conventional wisdom.

The death of Judah's wife was like an alarm clock for Tamar, telling her to rise and shine. It is of great importance that we recognize moments and times to shift for the better.

Verse 14 (Changing clothes)

"And she put her widow's garments off from her, and covered her with a vail, and wrapped herself, and sat in an open place, which is by the way to Timnath; for she saw that Shelah was grown, and she was not given to him to wife."

In order for a situation to change, you must do something different. Before, Tamar was simply going along with the flow of what was happening to her. She was told to go back to her father's house and remain a widow. So for a long period of time, Tamar dressed like a widow and consequently, she received the attention of a widow. She bore the stain of two dead men who had one thing in common: they both died while being married to her. Judah withheld Shelah because he feared that he would die also if married to Tamar. Sending Tamar back to her father's house with the shame of no child and two dead husbands would restrain her socially in the community. She was handcuffed by the perceptions of them that were around her. So many of us rely heavily on others to define who we. We cannot give them that much power. The only one able to do that is the one He who created you. The people around you can only define and describe you based off of what you have been through or what you are going through. God defines you on the purpose for which you were created. In this moment, you have to recognize that where you are in life will one day be a part of a "been through experience". You may be going through a shameful and troubling experience but the good news is that this place is NOT your final destination. You are going through to arrive at what God has purposed you for. Declare that my current situation is not my final dwelling place.

It's time to give the authority to define who you are, back to God. People will try to redefine you based on ideas and concepts of how they want you to be. They love who they desire for you to be but can't handle the reality of who you truly are. God's purpose for your life may literally scare and intimidate others who are insecure in themselves. You must rebel against every negative word against you. Take a stand and denounce what unauthorized people have pronounced over you. Anything spoken to you and over you that contradicts what God said about you is an attempt to hinder or stop you from success, production, and increase. Heb. 12:2 says that Jesus is the author and the finisher of our faith. It is up to us to make sure that He alone is writing the story.

The changing of clothes here in the text is symbolic of a change of heart or mentality. It is a mind shift. Her thoughts about herself changed, therefore her garments had to change. This is where a "made-up mind" is developed. Her experience told her that as long as I operate and live in these garments I will receive or attract what I am wearing. In other words, to some degree, you are responsible for what you attract. The behaviors you demonstrate and the way you present yourself have a huge impact on the way people behave around you. You must change your mind in order to properly embrace your divine opportunities. If God opens a door, please leave your old garments/old mentalities behind. It's time to change clothes. Your life will not change by chance it will change by choice. You have to choose to do, choose to grow, or choose to leave. Everything we do starts with a choice.

Much like Tamar, we need to evaluate our clothes (mentality). What has your mentality or way of thinking attracted? How has your current level of thinking affected your life? If you think the same way you will always experience the same people, same connections, and same results. The Bible says in Proverbs 23:7, *"as a man thinks, so is he."* We must choose to change our thoughts in order to become something greater. Life is too precious to waste time on negative thoughts. It's time to take control of your mind and your thoughts by watching what you allow to enter your ears and eyes. Many people lack control of their thoughts because they voluntarily allow so many outside influences to have power over the command center of their life. We devote countless hours to television shows that merely entertain without empowering us. The shows we watch, music we listen to, and people we spend time with all have some type of influence on our lives. This mix of influence helps to shape your world and your mind and has a large part to do with where you are in life currently. Some of your best friends may only be best friends because you are in the same situation. If you are not helping each other to be better then you are enabling each other to stay in the same situation. Remember, misery loves company.

What are the prevailing thoughts at the helms of your mind? It is up to us to determine which thoughts we will allow to rule in our soul. Things will begin to change once we realize that we are literally one thought and one decision away from a breakthrough.

Faith, Work, Prayer

Changing clothes is important to the reader because it shows that Tamar had to do something. All too often we sit back and expect Heaven to do all of the work because we decided to pray once or twice for a breakthrough or a miracle. Prayer is the communication to God that helps you receive strategy so that you can go and do. God gives us power, ability, and wisdom to accomplish things but none of those will work on the couch or while you are being still.

It's time to evolve into a go-getter, one who does not stay on the sideline but actively participates in the game. Nothing will work for you unless you work it. God has given you power so we do not depend on luck or superstition. As a believer in God we have to shun the "lottery mindset" and understand that God will bless the work of your hands. We have to do something. Doing nothing perpetuates the cycle of fruitlessness and barrenness. You have life for a reason. God has given you dreams, visions, plans, and ideas. It is your "doing" that will make the dream real and tangible. We have to move by faith and prayer in all things. Faith is not just a confession and prayer should not be some last resort after trying everything else. Praying by faith should be our first response, our first move.

The Bible says in James 5:16 that the effectual fervent prayer of the righteous availeth much. In other words your prayers accomplish great things. Why? Because of your faith in the one you are praying to. Prayer is the communication to God that releases the necessary strategy for change in your life. This is why 1 Thessalonians 5:16-18 encourages us to pray without ceasing. Prayer points us in the right direction and shows us how to apply our faith. Sometimes it seems like life can have us so completely drained and stressed that we don't even want to pray. We can feel so overwhelmed that we don't really have the words to say. It is in these moments and times that we should shut everything down and find a place to be transparent with God. Prayer through faith is our immediate connection to God. It is the cord that connects us to God who is our source of power. There are many distractions and negative forces that will try to interrupt the link of prayer in your life so it is up to you to make sure that prayer remains your most valuable asset. The good thing about prayer is that you can speak to God no matter what condition you are in, but the best part is that He will speak back!

Faith, prayer, and work are all needed in order to initiate and maintain a change in negative circumstances. Positive outcomes will occur when you pray according to His will and His word, not according to the flesh or our opinions. There are many things that you may want or desire but if those things will not be a necessity or benefit to the Kingdom of God, it may not be in line with His will for your life. We must remember that God will not deliver you simply to "do your own thing". For many of us doing our own thing is what caused us to be in bondage. God will deliver you from things that were designed to destroy you so that you will in turn help someone else to become free.

We must understand that God's main agenda is advancing His Kingdom. So our prayer should be, "God, bless me in a way that it will be a benefit to your Kingdom plan." When Jesus instructed His disciples to pray, he taught them to pray "thy Kingdome come, thy will be done" (Matthew 6:10). Many in today's church have gotten away from this prayer posture, but praying according to the Kingdom causes God to release answers, blessings, and divine help in any adverse situations. We do not have to complicate prayer. By faith, simply ask God, "What is your plan for my life?"

Tamar was able to overcome her father's house by seizing the moment. The death of Judah's wife presented an opportunity to change and she had to develop a plan or strategy. During this crucial time of planning, do not allow the opinions of others to ruin your divine opportunity. A God opportunity is a door that you have been properly processed to walk through. We don't know much about the history of Tamar but we can safely conclude that her eyes were open to opportunities to change her status and situation in life. She was able to recognize a door and did not let fear and doubt hold her back from walking through this door. For us, prayer and process is the key to discerning a divine opportunity to change. All too often people waste time wishing for things that they have not been properly processed for. Therefore, they are not ready to manage or maintain what they desire. There is a process for every prayer. There is a process to what you desire. One does not pray today to become great and tomorrow become great. The divine door will open once the process determines you are ready to walk through the door. In

Tamar's case, it was the process of Er, Onan, the failed promise of Shelah, and her father's house that prepared her for the death of Judah's wife. Once your prayer lines up with what you have been processed for, you will be able to realize when it's time to make a move.

Verse 14 also gives us another important key to Tamar's transformation. After Tamar changes out of her widows garments into a more attractive look. She went and sat in an open place. In other words, now that she had the look, it was time to be in the right location. It is not enough to look the part; we must be in the right position and location to be recognized. Some of us are all dressed up with no place to go. You must get to a place where people can appreciate what's on you. Not everyone will understand or be grateful for your gifts, anointing, and talents but God has a place and a people that will be affected by what He placed on you and in you. The enemy of your purpose desires for you to be clothed in sorrow, stagnation and fear. He knows that when your mentality changes towards the things of God, he will lose his influence and grip over your destiny. It's time to change clothes and go!

Tamar's attractive clothes would not garner the proper attention in her father's house. She had to leave to attract the right kind of person that would contribute to her goal of getting pregnant and changing her situation. We waste too much time trying to impress people who lack the ability or refuse to help us better ourselves. Could it be that the people you are around have no interest in your progress?

Genesis 38 says nothing of Tamar's background or of her family's role. The scriptures do not mention anything about Tamar's father but in those days it was the role of the father to arrange marriage of their children. Maybe Tamar's father had died or suffered some other fate that caused him to be absent in her life. The point of the matter is that she made no excuses as to why she should remain in a stuck place. Surely many of us could place blame on others for our current predicaments and downfalls. We could blame the absence of a father or the verbal abuse of a mother. We could even blame God for allowing bad things to happen that go beyond our understanding of His divine plan and will. The thing that will remain in the midst of us placing fault on people around us, however, is the situation that we are in if we make no effort toward the change we desire. Blaming others for where we are does not bring change, but responsibility for where you are going does. We all must overcome things beyond our control. Blaming others is only a temporary sedative while being in a permanent stuck position.

In verse 14, Tamar shows us the importance of relocation. In order to be productive, you may have to get away from familiar faces and places. You may have a hard time walking in your God-given purpose because of a connection to people with a limited view of who you are. If a person does not have high expectations for you, they will not invest much into you. I pray that God will surround us with people who can recognize the potential and the purpose that's on our lives. I pray that God will connect us to connected people that will help us do all that we are called to do. God will divinely connect you to people who will hold you accountable to what He said about you. There are people who are ordained to rehearse and repeat the promise in your ears until it comes to pass. The Ers and Onans won't do it. True friends will remind you of what God said and hold you to it.

Tamar's relocation process gave her opportunity and exposure. You will never get the opportunity to catch fish if you are afraid to be exposed to water. The open place where Tamar sat exposed her to opportunities that would alter her current condition. So, not only did she change clothes but she found a place that matched what she had on.

You wouldn't go work in a police department dressed in an astronaut suit. Tamar's attire was to attract and entice a man to want to engage and sleep with her. She knew that she had to have the right bait to catch the attention of Judah. There are times when we must evaluate ourselves. Is your lack of progress a result of having the wrong bait, bad location, or missed opportunities? I believe that through prayer, God will reveal any and all areas of a person's life that needs to change for the better.

8
TAMAR CONCEIVES
WITH JUDAH

> *Gen 38:16-18 – He turned to her at the roadside and said, "Come, let me come in to you," for he did not know that she was his daughter-in-law. She said, "What will you give me, that you may come in to me?" He answered, "I will send you a young goat from the flock." And she said, "If you give me a pledge, until you send it—" He said, "What pledge shall I give you?" She replied, "Your signet and your cord and your staff that is in your hand." So he gave them to her and went in to her, and she conceived by him.*

There are some people who will never believe you are ready for promotion or that you are ready to handle MORE but they have no idea how long you have been hidden and processed for divine exposure. Tamar's encounter with Er and Onan and even the long period of time she spent in her father's house was all a part of her process. Once you reach your "open place" of opportunities there will be those who will feel as if you do not deserve to be blessed. You must understand that because those around you are not present for every part of your process they will not fully understand the result or the reward of what you had to endure. The things you had to go through and the hardships you faced actually validate and qualify you for breakthrough. Many people abort the process and forfeit everything God has in store for them. In other words, when you understand that the things you are going through will cause you to become stronger and is the fulfillment of God's plan for your life, you will begin to operate in joy while you wait on God.

When Tamar sat in an open place it was not just taking advantage of a window of opportunity. Neither was it simply a move of desperation. In fact, it was a faith move. There will be times when the only thing you can do is move by faith.

When Judah saw Tamar, he did not know that she was his daughter-in-law but she knew exactly who he was. Tamar had something that Judah wanted but more importantly she knew the value of what Judah wanted from her. She could have tried to entice another man who may have passed through but she had an understanding and she knew who she was looking for. Once Judah saw her he asked if he could lay with her, which is exactly what she wanted to happen because her ultimate plan and desire was to get pregnant. Tamar does something more deliberate though. She asks him what would he give her before they slept together. So, Tamar sets herself up for more than pregnancy. She is trying to establish herself and change her situation permanently. Judah didn't have anything with him but he offers her a young goat from his flock which in those days would have been valuable for several reasons. Tamar accepts the goat but requires a pledge from Judah until she receives the goat. A pledge is something exchanged in the present moment as evidence that something else will be done. A pledge is like a security deposit that would be returned once a promise had been satisfied.

In verse 18, Judah sleeps with Tamar but not before she receives his signet (ring), chord (bracelet), and staff/rod, which have great symbolic meaning and gives us a dynamic strategy to make the best use of divine opportunities. Tamar shows us that we must first know our worth. Many people settle for a goat without asking for any security before you receive what is promised. Tamar knew that because of her worth she had to speak the language of the role that she was acting. Tamar was dressed like a harlot but was not about to walk away empty handed. Her experience with Onan had prepared her for this moment.

Learning from Tamar means that you understand how

to leverage your worth and not sell yourself short. Not only do you know how to look the part but you also know how to speak the language. Do you know how to negotiate? When God divinely sets you up for breakthrough, will you be properly prepared to make sure you take full advantage of the opportunity? God will open the door but it will be up to you to be prepared to walk through. Preparation includes, but it is not limited to, looking the part, knowing the language of the area you wish to impact, and being able to deliver what you promise. Being prepared also means being able negotiate what you will receive in exchange for your gifts, talents, and services rendered.

Tamar asked for the signet, bracelet, and staff because she knew that she would use these three items to prove that Judah was indeed the father. These items were especially distinct to Judah and represent many aspects of his life. All three objects represent the clout or influence of a person in a high ranking position.

The Signet

The signet that Judah gave to Tamar was used to put his own special mark on things that belonged to the owner of the signet. In those days, they made it in the form of a ring or seal that left an impression on anything owned by its wearer. Tamar knew that after her encounter with Judah, this particular symbol would show to everyone that she had been intimate with Judah. Judah in this text is a foreshadowing of Jesus Christ while Tamar represents what happens to all those who encounter Jesus with expectation. Much like Tamar, if we want to upgrade our lifestyle, we must become intimate with the one who has the ability to change our status. While in prayer, it's important for us to forsake the ritualistic mindset that causes the communication of a relationship to grow stale and cold. Many times we think we are going to God in prayer but actually we are only engaging in meaningless ceremonial activity that yields no real bond to God. In order to get to God, we must do it from the purity and sincerity of our hearts. Tamar was able to get to a place where Judah not only released seed but she left that encounter with evidence of who she had been with. There will always be some sign, both inward and outward, after an encounter with Jesus. Therefore, if we truly desire change, we must become intimate with Jesus to the point where we leave pregnant inwardly and marked outwardly. The seed that Jesus leaves in you will manifest to prove your relationship. The mark that Jesus leaves on you is a sign of his ownership. It's up to you to determine that every time you engage in communion with God that you will not leave empty handed.

The Chord

The chord or bracelet was worn by Judah and other shepherds on the arm or on other pieces of clothing. It was used to connect different pieces of clothing together. It was also used as a decorative ornament to represent rank within the community. As believers we must understand that the most important thing in our lives is our connection to God. By attaining the bracelet from Judah, Tamar now has an important object specific to Judah's clothes and covering. If a person were to see Tamar with this chord, they would know that Tamar was tied to Judah in some unique way. She was now in possession of the very thing that adorned Judah. In other words, through our connection to God, we should take on the same adornment of Christ. It is because of your connection to him that you will display some of the same attributes and characteristics. Christ was adorned and covered in humility, passion, and purpose. Even as Tamar covered herself with a veil and played the part of a harlot, Jesus as King of the Universe robed himself in humanity and played the part of a servant so that we would have the power and ability to be free from bondage. Our connection to Jesus causes us to be beautifully adorned with everything that He is (Psalm 149:4).

The Staff

The third thing Tamar asked for was Judah's staff or rod. Judah would have used his staff for several reasons, including walking, tending to sheep, and as a weapon against wild animals. The staff throughout scripture has been a symbol of the authority and might of God (Exodus 17:9-11). When we have an encounter with Jesus, we will leave empowered. There may be people who you are tied to now that cause you to feel drained and empty but being in the presence of God brings fulfillment and empowerment. I will even go as far to say that just because you go to church does not necessarily mean you have been in the presence of God. The presence of God has been noted scripturally and through experience to bring transformation, breakthrough, and power. From Genesis to Revelation, we see how people who were once weak and ineffectual experienced the presence of God and became empowered to perform great feats. You can, and oftentimes will, experience God in places outside of a church building. God is immensely larger than the four walls of a local assembly and should not be limited to one particular place or space.

God will grant authority to those who are willing to step outside of the ceremonial bondage of who we want Him to be and connect with him through unrehearsed communion. With the authority of God you literally have the backing and approval of God. The authority of God gives clearance and access to perform and operate in divine purpose. We absolutely need the authority of God in order to be effective and to change any negative situation we may be in. It is the authority of His word that is able to change us and our circumstances.

So, how do I know my situation will change? I know it will change because God has placed his stamp of approval on me and vested authority in me. It's time we take a firm hold of the rod that God has given us and walk boldly to fulfill what he placed in us. When Moses felt weak and incapable of completing his God-given assignment, the Lord spoke from a burning bush and asked, *"What is in your hand?"* Moses responded saying, *"a staff"* (Exodus 4:1-5). God was letting Moses know that He would be with him in the face of Pharaoh and that he did not have to fear. God said to Moses that the staff would be a tool to prove that God had appeared before Moses (Exodus 4:5). Remember the rod was used for walking and for protection. God will help you to perform His plan, which is your purpose, and he will protect you from opposing forces as the plan unfolds in your life.

Judah

The name Judah is the Hebrew word 'Yehudah' which means praise. This time Tamar became intimate with a man whose name meant praise. Praise is a key element to breakthrough and advancement because it is an indication of our faith. Oftentimes we hear that praise is a weapon against the enemy. I would add that praise is the faithful response to the word and promises of God regardless of the fiery trial you may be in presently. So often we find ourselves in storms and issues that are contrary to what God said about us. It is in these times that our faith is revealed, mostly through our ability to give God praise. Tamar's intimate activity with Judah (praise) can be seen as the catalyst that ushers her to the desired goal. Just like prayer, praise must be done from the heart. Praise is directly connected to your faith. Therefore, if there is no faith in your heart there will be no true praise from your heart. No one else can force you to praise God. As a matter of fact, praise is a function of your own will. You have to determine within yourself that you will praise God no matter what may be happening in your life.

David experienced many hardships and trials in his life but he vowed to bless the Lord at all times (Psalm 34:1). This speaks to a lifestyle of faith and praise. Your breakthrough may be held up because of a lack of faith and an inconsistent "praise life". Praise is the act of giving him thanks for what He has done in your life and for what you are expecting Him to do. Praise causes you to declare to others how awesome God is in your life despite how it may seem (Psalm 34:2). There are countless reasons to praise God. Tamar gives us at least three reasons. While in His presence, we can praise him for identification, divine connection, and authority.

Tamar shows us that we will have to spiritually conceive through praise, which causes us to be open and receptive to the seed God wants to release in us while we are in His presence. When you decide to forsake surface level praise and worship and devote all of your being to His will then he will release and cause you to become pregnant with strategy, vision, and power.

9
THERE'S SOMETHING ABOUT TAMAR

Gen. 38:27-30 – Now it came to pass, at the time for giving birth, that behold, twins were in her womb. And so it was, when she was giving birth, that the one put out his hand; and the midwife took a scarlet thread and bound it on his hand, saying, "This one came out first." Then it happened, as he drew back his hand, that his brother came out unexpectedly; and she said, "How did you break through? This breach be upon you!" Therefore his name was called Perez. Afterward his brother came out who had the scarlet thread on his hand. And his name was called Zerah.

After Tamar's meeting with Judah, they go their separate ways. Judah sends his friend with a goat to deliver to Tamar as promised. When Judah's friend arrives to meet her, she is not there and the friend cannot find her. Genesis 38:21 says that the people of that place said there was no harlot ever in the area. Judah decides to simply let her keep the signet, chord, and staff in order to refrain from causing too much attention to his situation.

Three months later, Tamar obviously begins to show that she is pregnant and word gets back to Judah that his daughter-in-law has done something immoral. She is not married but she is pregnant. In those days this was a horrible offense. His decision is swift and to the point. His judgment is that she be burned for her wrongdoing. What he does not know is that Tamar is the harlot he encountered about three months earlier. Tamar presents the signet, chord, and staff and says the owner of these items is the father. This is one of the most controversial paternity tests of all time. Judah had to admit that he had unknowingly slept with Tamar. He understood that she had tricked him because he had not followed through on his promise to marry her to his son Shelah. Her ability to prove that Judah was the father literally saved her life and the life of what was inside her womb. Surely we should all know by now that we experience conflict not merely based on who we are but also because of what we are carrying. There are attacks that come because of who you are connected to and then there is conflict because of what is on the inside of you. You will experience spiritual warfare simply because of what you are able to produce. The people around Tamar were getting ready to destroy her because of how she got pregnant. It wasn't until she presented the signet, chord, and rod that they understood who was responsible for her pregnancy.

This is comforting to the reader of this passage of scripture because it shows us that the one who has invested spiritual seed in us is also able to confirm that he is the father. God is not a silent partner or one who simply releases seed in your life only to then neglect you. The "who" in Tamar's process outweighed all other factors. Jesus is not only our greatest investor; He is our ultimate Savior and consistent protector. Our very lifestyle should produce evidence of who we have been in contact with. When people look at you, are they able to tell who you are connected to? The authority and favor that you walk in confirms your relationship to God. There will most certainly be times where you are confronted like Tamar because of what you are about to produce. In those moments simply operate in the divine identity of Christ, focus on your divine connection to God, and use your authority because the greatest power is backing you up.

In your time of changing, people will see different phases of your process. When your pregnancy begins to show, some who will become jealous or envious of you simply because there is evidence that you have been actively working to get better. Please understand that there will be times when you are the only one fighting for your freedom from stagnation. When it became evident to others that Tamar was pregnant, it was a sign of progress. It was an indication of where her life was going. We cannot allow the opinions of those who refuse to change for the better to distract us from what God has spoken over our lives. You must fight for freedom and become comfortable with fighting alone sometimes.

The Labor and Travail of Tamar

There are many people who have discovered that what God has called them to, goes above and beyond what they had in mind when they first came into the knowledge of their purpose. There really is no way to fully understand the totality of all that God has placed in you simply because God's thoughts and ways are above ours (Isaiah 55:8-9). As you grow in your relationship with God, you grow in faith and trust. You may not understand everything He is doing in your life or even how or why but you will know that all things are working together for you because you love God and are called according to His purpose (Romans 8:28).

When it was time to give birth, Tamar discovered twins. I must encourage you by letting you know that your time of reward will be greater than your time of struggle and heartbreak! God has a way of overwhelming you with blessings to the point where the things you went through shrink in comparison to where he takes you. When it comes time to give birth to your purpose, you will begin to understand why you had to endure everything you experienced. The announcement of twins to Tamar is confirmation to us that what we are going through now will be worth it to operate in purpose. Your endurance in the process and operation of purpose brings glory to God. All of your struggles, times of rejection, and spiritual warfare causes you to bring God glory. Paul had this to say about what you are going through right now: *"For I reckon that the sufferings of this present time are not worthy to be compared with the glory which shall be revealed in us"* (Romans 8:18). It doesn't matter what others might be saying or doing around you. Keep pressing and you will find that because of the glory, your God ordained hardships will not be able to be compared to what you will produce.

Times of birth and labor are indications that you were able to carry and feed the purpose of God without aborting or quitting under pressure. Not only is it important to become aware of who you are and what is in you but you also have to be able to cause growth to the seed. In other words, you have to put yourself in positions to nurture what is in you.

How do I feed and cause growth to my purpose? When it comes to breakthrough and fulfilling God's plan for your life there must be plans of protection to safe guard and guarantee a healthy delivery. We know that when a woman finds out that she is pregnant, she is advised to cut out alcohol and be careful of taking certain medications. These precautions are strongly advised so that the health of the baby and the mother is not jeopardized and so that there can be a healthy delivery. To protect your gifts and purpose, you must stay away from things that distort your mind. Many people are gifted but operate "under the influence" of things that are not connected to the will or plan of God. When you consume things that negatively affect who you are and what you possess, it will cause you to produce something that may be premature and under developed. Growth can occur by simply abstaining from people and places that are contrary to the giver of the gift. Also, growth happens when you consistently consume the Word of God. He will continue to reveal the dynamics of what He placed in you while providing divine wisdom as to how to carry out His plan for your life. You have to consider the things you allow to enter your mind. A steady diet of prayer, studying and believing His Word, meditation, fasting, praise and worship all help to ensure healthy growth and production. There are many things that threaten the growth and development of your "baby" but God will give you the ability to carry it. It is your responsibility to cautiously and spiritually monitor the things you consume.

To push something out, there must first be some type of planting or impregnation. In other words, there can be no travail if there is no pregnancy. Oftentimes in the church people are encouraged to "travail in the Spirit." To travail means you have reached the point of giving birth after carrying a thing for a long period of time. Travail involves carrying a burden or load while experiencing intense internal pain. It has often been associated with sounds of agony, wailing, and moaning. It should be noted that travail has more to do with the work and toil it takes to produce or manage what God has placed in your care.

You, like Tamar, may be in a time of great travail. It may even seem like the pain you feel has brought you close to the very gates of death. There was a great seed placed in you and there will be great affliction and warfare even up to your time to give birth. Travail is common for those who have been with God and plan to complete the assignment

He put in them. You will survive the pain and push out the vision, ministry, business, and everything God has for you will come to pass.

Tamar's Connection

We are all connected to Tamar. Tamar may not be the most memorable Biblical figure but her contribution and work in the plan of God is huge. After Genesis 38, this particular Tamar is not mentioned again until Matthew Chapter 1.

The Genealogy of Jesus Christ

1The book of the genealogy of Jesus Christ, the son of David, the son of Abraham. 2Abraham was the father of Isaac, and Isaac the father of Jacob, and Jacob the father of Judah and his brothers, 3and Judah the father of Perez and Zerah by Tamar, and Perez the father of Hezron, and Hezron the father of Ram...

Verse 3 shows that the lineage from Perez (the twin that came out first) leads to Jesus Christ. Everything Tamar endured was not just for her but it connects us all to the one who redeems. Tamar was a normal woman in a society where women were not treated well but she was tasked with a divine assignment to produce greatness. Never think that you are insignificant or that your gifts will not impact the lives of others. Tamar's pregnancy impacts us all. People may try to manipulate you into to believing that you are not great but understand you are fearfully and wonderfully made. Whatever God has purposed for you to carry and produce will cause positive impact for the Kingdom of God.

Tamar's experience is an encouraging one. Through her life we see that we have the power and ability to shift the course of our lives with a decision. The people around Tamar obviously thought very little of her. Error, Onan, Shelah, and Judah all had no idea that little known Tamar would be a great figure in the genealogy of our Lord and Savior. I believe there was a driving force behind Tamar's boldness and strategic moves. There was something about Tamar that would not allow her to simply accept what was handed to her. Many people would have allowed bitterness, regret, and anger to restrict their forward advancement. Tamar, however, decided to use every setback and disappointment to become her motivation for change. We must learn to use every negative experience as a reason to keep pushing. God will give you the ability to recognize defining moments in your life. Many people have allowed bad situations to force them into bad choices. That will NOT be you. You will NOT make a bad decision in a key moment. You will recognize and submit to the move of God in your life!

JON SHORTEREZ

10
IT'S TIME TO GO

One stormy morning, while getting ready for work, I tried to wait on the rain to stop or lighten up before leaving. The moment I settled my mind on the decision, I heard the Lord simply say, "If you wait you will be late." I automatically knew that what was spoken to me was not just concerning being tardy to work. When God speaks to you, it will hit and effect every part of your being. The spirit within me began to minister to my mind as I quickly ran from the house, through the rain to my car. The Lord was saying that if you wait on the rain to stop in your life you will rarely move forward and be subject to stagnation. Many of us have missed out on great opportunities all because we felt like there was a lot going on in our lives. You do not have time to wait on certain things to improve or certain people to change. Waiting on others unnecessarily will diminish your value and stall your purpose. To subject yourself to a person or situation when you do not have to, will lead to future frustration and regret. When your mind is truly made up, rain, sleet, or snow will not stop you from success.

The rain represents the constant friction and conflict that is associated with your purpose. It seems as if every time you take one step forward something happens that knocks you backwards. A death in the family, medical bills, divorce, wayward children, even a flat tire can be "rain" in your life. But God will be the driving force on your path to victory and breakthrough. The rain is normal for the course you are on. If you are waiting on things to quiet and slow down before making a move, you are not ready to embrace your purpose or handle the weight of responsibility that is connected to your assignment. If it wasn't for the rain, many of us would not have any type of consistent prayer life. It is our struggles that often cause us to pray with fervency and urgency. The trials we endure mold and shape us spiritually and actually causes maturity in God. The rain makes us more familiar with the voice of God and sensitive to the way He operates in our lives. It is while pressing through hard times and tight spots that God develops character and integrity while causing you to walk with humility. So, while your situation is changing for the better, go ahead and thank God for breakthrough but never forget what you had to go through.

Go ahead and fill out the job application, research the steps to start that business, go back to school, create a workout plan to live a healthier lifestyle, but most importantly, follow through!

I received a divine push that day while getting ready for work. It was actually bringing me to the reality of my situation. If I wait on the rain to cease, I may be dry but I would arrive late. If I press through the rain I arrive on time. Years from now the last thing you want to say is that rain held you back from changing your circumstance. Come to the understanding and realization that you will just have to get wet but you will not be held back. You will be frustrated and uncomfortable at times by the process of change but you will not be held back. There will be setbacks in your life and moving forward will not always be comfortable or seemingly favorable but if your mind is made up, you will press through. Determine right now that you will not be late to what God has called you to, even if you have to show up soaking wet.

In Genesis Chapter 38, Tamar shows us that no matter how things are stacked against you, you can change. You have the ability to take control of your current circumstance in order to have a positive effect on your future. You may have gone through a season of mistakes and poor execution of plans but through your connection to God and the power of your choices, you can fix your fate. Your life is a culmination of everything you have allowed into your spirit. If you change what you allow in, the outcome of your life will turn for the better.

It is my prayer that you will connect to the greatest power, which is the Lord Jesus. It is then that you will see that the benefits of change far outweigh the challenges of change. Your breakthrough will positively affect many generations after you.

JON SHORTEREZ

ABOUT THE AUTHOR

Jon Shorterez is an ordained minister from Houston, Texas. He was called to the ministry at the age of 12. After studying business administration at the University of North Texas, Shorterez is currently pursuing a degree in Christian counseling from Liberty University. An anointed gospel teacher, revivalist and ministry strategist, Shorterez, attends Latter House Glory Tabernacle, where he serves as senior minister for Pastor Elton Monday. In his spare time, he enjoys traveling with his wife, Courtney, writing and coaching a Select Summer Basketball team called the North Texas Wolves. Jon and his wife reside in the Dallas-Fort Worth area of Texas.

Follow him on social media.
Facebook: Jon Rafeal Shorterez
Instagram: @radicalremnant
Email: jonshorterez@gmail.com

FOR MORE TITLES FROM EX3 BOOKS

VISIT OUR WEBSITE AT:
www.EX3BOOKS.com

Feel free to leave reviews about
I Choose Breakthrough
on our website, email info@ex3books.com, or
at Amazon.com.

www.ingramcontent.com/pod-product-compliance
Lightning Source LLC
Chambersburg PA
CBHW052150090426
42741CB00010B/2207